DATE DUE

7.96

JY 23 '88	MY 23 '92	26	
OC 6 '88	16 '92	29	
NO 10 '88	OCT 16		
JY 20 '88	OCT 26		
AG 17 '88	MAY 07		
NO 21 '89	FEB 13		
JY 12 '90	JUN 11		
JY 23 '90	JUN 19		
AG 16 '90	NOV 06		
DE 1 '90	JY 21 '99		
JY 29 '91	JY 15		
AP 16 '92	DE 10 '05		

E
Sti

Stiles, Norman
The Count's number
parade

The COUNT'S Number Parade

by Norman Stiles

illustrated by Joe Veno

featuring Jim Henson's Muppets

A SESAME STREET BOOK

Published by Western Publishing Company, Inc. in conjunction with Children's Television Workshop. © 1977 Children's Television Workshop. The Count and other Muppet characters © 1973, 1977 Muppets, Inc. All rights reserved. Printed in U.S.A.

Tenth Printing, 1980

Greetings and welcome to
my fabulous Number Parade!

It's beginning!
That's one.
1 baton twirler!

And one, two . . .

2 dancing elephants!

One, two,
three, four . . .

4 smiling bass-drum players!

One, two, three, four, five . . .

5 wonderful
upside-down violin players!

One, two, three, four, five, six . . .

6 whistling bananas!

One, two, three, four,
five, six, seven . . .
7 flute-playing octopuses
in sneakers!

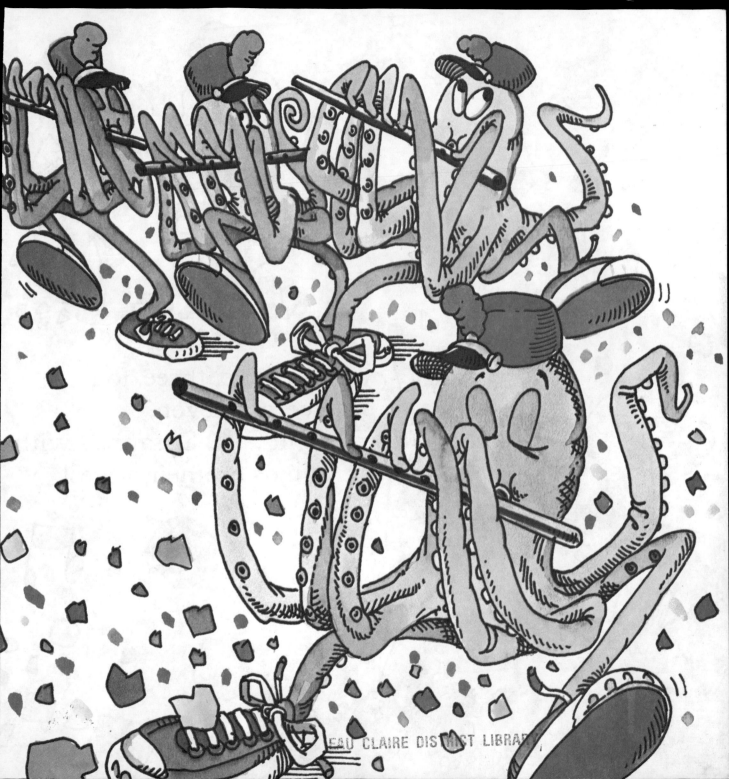

One, two, three, four,
five, six, seven,
eight . . . **8** Susannas with
banjos on their knees!

One, two, three, four,
five, six, seven, eight,
nine ... **9** horses!

And last but not least—
one, two, three, four,
five, six, seven, eight,
nine, ten . . . **10** tuba-playing
Twiddlebugs!

Oh, I loved counting that parade. And do you know what I love counting after I count parades?